CHICAGO PUBLIC LIBRARY
BUSINESS / SCIENCE / TECHNOLOGY
400 S. STATE ST.     60605

# PROFILES IN MATHEMATICS

## Carl Friedrich Gauss

# Profiles in Mathematics:

# Carl Friedrich Gauss

Krista West

MORGAN
REYNOLDS
PUBLISHING

Greensboro, North Carolina

R0423185077

CHICAGO PUBLIC LIBRARY
BUSINESS /SCIENCE/TECHNOLOGY
400 S. STATE ST.
CHICAGO IL 60605

# Profiles in
# Mathematics:

**Alan Turing**

**Rene' Descartes**

**Carl Friedrich Gauss**

**Sophie Germain**

**Pierre de Fermat**

**Ancient Mathematicians**

**Women Mathematicians**

PROFILES IN MATHEMATICS
CARL FRIEDRICH GAUSS

Copyright © 2009 By Krista West

All rights reserved.
This book, or parts thereof, may not be reproduced in any form
except by written consent of the publisher. For more information write:
Morgan Reynolds Publishing, Inc., 620 South Elm Street, Suite 223
Greensboro, North Carolina 27406 USA

Library of Congress Cataloging-in-Publication Data

West, Krista.
    Carl Friedrich Gauss / by Krista West.
        p. cm. -- (Profiles in mathematics)
    Includes bibliographical references and index.
    ISBN-13: 978-1-59935-063-9
    ISBN-10: 1-59935-063-7
    1.  Gauss, Carl Friedrich, 1777-1855. 2.
Mathematicians--Germany--Biography. I. Title.
    QA29.G3W47 2008
    510.92--dc22
    [B]
                                2008018486

Printed in the United States of America
First Edition

*To my math-minded husband, whose own use of math to understand our world has helped me appreciate its value*

# Contents

# Introduction

Mathematics gives us a powerful way to analyze and try to understand many of the things we observe around us, from the spread of epidemics and the orbit of planets, to grade point averages and the distance between cities. Mathematics also has been used to search for spiritual truth, as well as the more abstract question of what is knowledge itself.

Perhaps the most intriguing question about mathematics is where does it come from? Is it discovered, or is it invented? Does nature order the world by mathematical principles, and the mathematician's job is to uncover this underlying system? Or is mathematics created by mathematicians as developing cultures and technologies require it? This unanswerable question has intrigued mathematicians and scientists for thousands of years and is at the heart of this new series of biographies.

The development of mathematical knowledge has progressed, in fits and starts, for thousands of years. People from various areas and cultures have discovered new mathematical concepts and devised complex systems of algorithms and equations that have both practical and philosophical impact.

To learn more of the history of mathematics is to encounter some of the greatest minds in human history. Regardless of whether they were discoverers or inventors, these fascinating lives are filled with countless memorable stories—stories filled with the same tragedy, triumph, and persistence of genius as that of the world's great writers, artists, and musicians.

Knowledge of Pythagoras, René Descartes, Carl Friedrich Gauss, Sophie Germain, Alan Turing, and others will help to lift mathematics off the page and out of the calculator, and into the minds and imaginations of readers. As mathematics becomes more and more ingrained in our day-to-day lives, awakening students to its history becomes especially important.

Sharon F. Doorasamy
Editor in chief

## *Editorial Consultant*

In his youth, Curt Gabrielson was inspired by reading the biographies of dozens of great mathematicians and scientists. "I was driven to learn math when I was young, because math is the language of physical science," says Curt, who named his dog Archimedes. "I now know also that it stands alone, beautiful and mysterious." He learned the more practical side of mathematics growing up on his family's hog farm in Missouri, designing and building structures, fixing electrical systems and machines, and planning for the yearly crops.

After earning a BS in physics from MIT and working at the San Francisco Exploratorium for several years, Curt spent two years in China teaching English, science, and math, and two years in Timor-Leste, one of the world's newest democracies, helping to create the first physics department at the country's National University, as well as a national teacher-training program. In 1997, he spearheaded the Watsonville Science Workshop in northern California, which has earned him recognition from the U.S. Congress, the California State Assembly, and the national Association of Mexican American educators. Mathematics instruction at the Workshop includes games, puzzles, geometric construction, and abacuses.

Curt Gabrielson is the author of several journal articles, as well as the book *Stomp Rockets, Catapults, and Kaleidoscopes: 30+ Amazing Science Projects You Can Build for Less than $1.*

Carl Friedrich Gauss

# one
# Child Genius

In March 1796, near the German town of Brunswick, nineteen-year-old (Johann) Carl Friedrich Gauss made a discovery that had eluded mathematicians for two millennia. The ancient Greeks had known how to construct regular polygons with five and ten sides, using a ruler and compass, and Euclid of Alexandria, one of the greatest mathematicians of antiquity, had constructed fifteen-sided polygons (pentadecagons). But no one had thought it possible to construct a regular polygon with seventeen sides (a heptadecagon).

Gauss, the son of a common laborer, not only proved that this geometrical construction was possible, but before reaching the age of twenty-five he would make many more mathematical breakthroughs. Gauss considered the discovery of the heptadecagon his greatest, and it is the one that convinced him to enter the field of mathematics. Until then,

*Euclid*

Euclid, an ancient mathematician from Alexandria, had constructed polygons with fifteen sides, but Gauss was the first person to construct a seventeen-sided polygon. *(Courtesy of Classic Image/Alamy)*

he had not known what he would do to earn a living, an uncertainty that had prompted his mother to ask what would become of him. When one of Gauss's closest friends assured her that Gauss would become "Europe's greatest mathematician," she cried.

It was clear from an early age that Carl Friedrich Gauss was a mathematical genius. Born April 30, 1777, Carl taught himself to read and write by the age of three. In his old age, he often repeated to friends and acquaintances that he had learned to do mental calculations before he had learned to talk.

Gauss was born in this house in 1777.

Carl's parents were hard-working but poor; neither had much, if any, formal schooling, and they spoke a local dialect that reflected their status as peasant-laborers in German society. Carl's father, Gebhard Dietrich Gauss, worked as a bricklayer, gardener, canal-tender, street butcher, and as an accountant for a funeral society. Carl's mother, Dorothea Benze, had worked as a maid for seven years before marrying Gebhard. She was one year older than her husband, who had a son, Johann George Heinrich, from a previous marriage. Gebhard's first wife had died in 1775.

Brunswick, a city in northern Germany in the duchy of Brunswick, was nestled between the Oker River and the Harz Mountains. Carl and his parents lived in a small house near an open canal which joined the Oker, a river that flowed through

A nineteenth-century view of Brunswick, Germany *(Library of Congress)*

the center of Brunswick. As a little boy, Carl once fell into the canal, but was saved before drowning. The house was the family's means to full citizenship in Brunswick, which at the time was considered the cultural and political capital of the duchy. The town was home to some 20,000 residents, and many had migrated there from outlying farming areas hoping for a better life. Gebhard Gauss's grandfather was one of those migrants. He had settled in the city around 1740 and purchased a house in 1753. Without ownership of a home, residents could not claim the full rights and privileges of citizenship.

Dorothea, known for her strong character, wit, intelligence, and fondness for plain blue linen dresses, recognized early on that there was something special about her only child. One day, Gebhard was busy calculating the weekly payroll for some of the men with whom he worked. Young Carl stood by, quietly adding and subtracting in his head, while his father added a long column of numbers on paper. Unaware that his son was paying attention, Gebhard was surprised when young Carl spoke up and said, "Father, the reckoning is wrong." Gebhard Gauss checked his calculations and found that his three-year-old son was correct.

## Calculating the Date of Easter

One of Carl's earliest discoveries was the day of his own birth. His mother only knew that he had been born on a Wednesday, eight days before the Ascension in the year 1777. To figure out his actual birth date, Carl wrote a mathematical formula to calculate the date of Easter in any year, and then he calculated his birthday.

Carl knew that the Ascension is the fortieth day after Easter. To get the exact date of his birth, he first had to figure out the date of Easter in that year and then count backwards. But the date of Easter, it turns out, is complicated.

The date of Easter is different every year, but it always falls on the first Sunday after the first full moon after the start of spring (when the days begin to get longer). Easter, then, is determined by two things: the phase of the moon (whether the moon is full or not) and the length of the day (whether the day is getting longer or shorter).

If these two things are known for the year, the date of Easter can be calculated. Carl consulted many old calendars, and in about a week he wrote a set of formulas that can be used to calculate the date of Easter in any given year. You start with the year and do the following calculations:

| | |
|---|---|
| Year divided by 4 | Remainder = a |
| Year divided by 7 | Remainder = b |
| Year divided by 7 | Remainder = c |
| $\dfrac{19c+M}{30}$ | Remainder = d |
| $\dfrac{2a + 4b + 6d + N}{7}$ | Remainder = e |
| $22 + d + e =$ <br> $d + e - 9 =$ | Date in March <br> Date in April |

When Carl reached age seven, Gebhard Gauss reluctantly permitted him to attend school. At the time, a formal education was not mandatory, and neither was attendance strictly enforced. Children were expected to work in the home and learn a trade (such as carpentry or blacksmithing) to help support the family. It was common for boys to attend school for a few years to learn basic reading, writing, and arithmetic, but any education past age fifteen was considered a waste of time for non-aristocrats. Most girls did not attend school at all.

Gebhard enrolled his son in St. Katharine's in 1784. More than one hundred boys of various ages crammed into the school, which had a low ceiling, uneven floors, and was musty and dark. For the first two years of Carl's formal education, he was a student of J. G. Büttner, who used a whip to keep order in the classroom—a practice not uncommon for that era.

One day Büttner gave the class what he thought was a brainteaser. He asked the class to write down all the whole numbers from 1 to 100 and add up their sum. The first boy to finish was expected to write down his answer on a slate board and lay it on a table. The other students would follow by laying their slates on top of the first one, and so on.

Carl calculated the correct answer almost instantly. He turned in his slate, saying *"Ligget se.* (There it is.)" When asked to defend his answer, young Carl explained to Büttner that instead of adding all the numbers individually, as the other students were doing, he saw a pattern in pairs of numbers. Astonished, Büttner realized that Carl was no ordinary student.

Büttner ordered advanced textbooks from Hamburg for his young student, and he arranged for him to start work-

# Number Patterns

Nearly all modern biographies of Carl Friedrich Gauss tell the story of how, at age of about nine or ten, he almost instantly recognized that the sum of the integers from 1 to 100 is 5,050. Whether or not the story is true is the subject of wide speculation. Nevertheless, there is a lesson to be learned from the exercise that Büttner gave his students: recognizing patterns is important. Young Carl Gauss rapidly recognized the symmetry of the mathematical problem, and he showed Büttner his pattern of paired numbers:

$$100 + 1 = 101$$
$$99 + 2 = 101$$
$$98 + 3 = 101$$
$$\cdot$$
$$\cdot$$
$$\cdot$$
$$48 + 53 = 101$$
$$49 + 52 = 101$$
$$50 + 51 = 101$$

Carl created fifty pairs of numbers that each added up to 101, using all the numbers from 1 to 100 only once. 50 x 101 gives the sum of the numbers from 1 to 100 without performing the long addition, and according to the story, that's how young Carl arrived at 5,050.

ing with a tutor, Johann Christian Martin Bartels, who later became a professor of mathematics at the University of Kazan in Russia. Bartels was a neighbor and eight years older than Carl. The son of a pewterer, he had a personal interest in mathematics and became an early friend to Carl. The two liked to take long walks together when not studying.

It did not take long for Carl to surpass his tutor. Bartels and Büttner realized that they needed to have a conversation with Gebhard Gauss about Carl's future. They knew that Carl had great potential as a mathematician, but Gebhard wanted his son to become a laborer to help support the family. Already, he had arranged an evening job for his son: spinning flax into yarn.

Gebhard Gauss was "honest," "well-regarded," and "in many ways worthy of respect," but he could be "tyrannical" and "coarse." He did not fully appreciate his son's mathematical abilities, or understand how his son could make a decent wage from his talents. For Gebhard Gauss, life was a constant struggle, and earning enough to supply his family's most basic needs was an ever-present concern.

Johann Christian Martin Bartels, Gauss's math tutor

Nevertheless, Bartels and Büttner somehow convinced Gebhard to allow Carl to spend his evenings studying, rather than spinning. The young scholar would study late into the night, by the light of a candle he made by hollowing out a turnip and filling it with kitchen fat leftover from his mother's cooking. Carl would then take a scrap of rolled cotton, soak it in the fat, and light the piece of cloth.

Bartels and Büttner knew that one day Carl would need financial assistance to continue his studies, and it was clear that Gebhard could not afford such an expense. So Bartels and Büttner began talking to influential people in Brunswick about their prized student. Both seemed certain that they could "find some distinguished person or protector or patron for such a genius."

# two
# Finding Independence

**B**üttner and Bartels knew that Carl had extraordinary talents and wanted to study math if a way to pay for it could be found. His half-brother George eventually would follow in his father's footsteps and work as a laborer, and Carl was expected to do the same.

Carl lived during a time when England and other parts of Europe were moving from primarily agricultural and rural economies to urban, industrial ones, though the duchy of Brunswick and other small German states seemed slow to progress in this direction. Brunswick had once been a prosperous city because of its location at the intersection of several important trade routes and the Oker River. The Oker flowed from north to south right through the center of the city, and its tributaries provided navigable water routes that stretched to the city of Bremen as well as to the North Sea. By the time Carl was born, however, the city had deteriorated, weakened by revolts and wars. Old, wealthy families had abandoned the town, while immigrants from nearby villages had begun settling there in large numbers, including Carl's family.

The world beyond Brunswick was rapidly changing, too. A new nation, the United States, had been formed across the ocean in 1776, the year before Carl's birth, and the French Revolution began when Carl was twelve. Kings had ruled France for a thousand years, but the French people had grown

A scene from the French Revolution in 1789. *(Courtesy of Visual Arts Library (London)/Alamy)*

restless for change: the French government was bankrupt, and many groups blamed the royals and wanted an end to the monarchy's powerful rule. Eventually, the armies of France would invade Brunswick, but by then Carl would have made most of his groundbreaking advances in math and science.

In 1788, with nothing further to learn at Büttner's school, Bartels and Büttner helped Carl gain entrance to the Gymnasium Catharineum, a college preparatory school located only a couple of miles from Carl's home. There he exhibited a talent for languages, including High German, which was considered superior to the local dialect that he spoke at home. It wasn't long, though, before Carl distinguished himself as a student of math. Professor Hellwig, the math professor, returned Carl's first written report, noting that Carl's knowledge of math was so advanced that there was no need for him to attend his lectures.

That same year Bartels enrolled at the Collegium Carolinum, a relatively new institution that had gained a reputation as a progressive, science-oriented academy. Founded and run by the Brunswick government ten years earlier, the Collegium was located in a three-story-high stone building and boasted a large, well-endowed library. Bartels's family had come to know many professors at the institution, in particular Eberhard A. W. Zimmermann, a highly respected professor of mathematics, physics, and natural history.

Bartels arranged for Zimmermann to meet Carl, and in 1791 Zimmerman, who was also a high civil servant, arranged for fourteen-year-old Carl to meet the duke of Brunswick, Charles William Ferdinand. The duke was an enlightened monarch—well-educated and cultured, he had traveled widely

Charles William Ferdinand, the duke of Brunswick, funded Gauss's education.

and was a supporter of academics and the arts. After meeting Carl, the duke granted him a yearly stipend of ten thalers, an amount sufficient to cover tuition and living expenses at the Collegium Carolinum. Carl began his studies at the Collegium in 1792 at age fifteen, and would remain there for the next three years.

Zimmerman determined there was no need for Carl to take math classes because he already knew all the subject matter. Instead, Carl spent time learning more about the history of math and refining his use of Latin and Greek.

Carl studied the works of three prominent mathematicians: Leonhard Euler, Joseph Louis Lagrange, and Isaac Newton. Euler was a Swiss mathematician (1707–1783) famous for writing more volumes on the subject than anyone else. He helped develop calculus, introduced many of the mathematical symbols in use today, and explored the concept of infinity. Lagrange was an Italian-French mathematician (1736–1813) who specialized in Number Theory and pure math. But it was Newton (1643–1727), the English mathematician, physicist, and philosopher who most impressed Carl. Newton

Newton's use of math to explore the forces in the universe made a lasting impression on Gauss during his studies at the Collegium Carolinum. *(Courtesy of Mary Evans Picture Library/Alamy)*

Leonhard Euler
*(Courtesy of The Print
Collector/Alamy)*

Joseph Louis Lagrange
*(Courtesy of Classic Image/Alamy)*

explored the forces in the universe with math. He was the first to show that the force keeping the moon in orbit around the earth (gravity) was the same force that caused an apple to fall from a tree. He wrote many laws of motion, helped create calculus, explored the speed of sound, and proved that white light was made of many colors.

For the first time in his life, the rich history of mathematics was at Carl's fingertips in the Collegium Carolinum's prestigious library, and it appears he spent much of his time studying these historical texts. At the same time, Carl was learning about the most current research in the field of math. By his final year at the Collegium Carolinum, Carl had discovered what is known as the Method of Least Squares.

Although he discovered the Method of Least Squares in 1795, when he was only eighteen years old, Carl didn't formally published this work until 1809. This delay in publishing became a characteristic of Carl's work. He only published his ideas when two criteria were met: he had thoroughly investigated the idea, and he felt the field of mathematics was ready to hear what he had to say. Over time, he would adopt the motto, *pauca sed matura* ("few but ripe").

The French mathematician Adrien-Marie Legendre (1752–1833) was the first person to formally publish the Method of Least Squares in 1805. Because of this publication, Legendre sometimes gets the credit for discovering this method.

During his time at the Collegium Carolinum, Carl developed a solid understanding of what was already known in the world of math. Soon he would make his own contributions to the field, and establish his place in history as one of the most profound and inventive mathematicians of his time.

# The Method of Least Squares

The Least Squares Method is one of the oldest techniques of modern statistics. To understand this method, imagine using a ruler to measure a line on a piece of paper. No matter how careful you are to get the correct measurement, you are likely to come up with a different length of line each time it is measured. If you measure the line ten times, for example, you might get a list of measurements that looks like this:

| Measurement No. | Length of Line |
|---|---|
| Measurement 1 | 6.2 cm |
| Measurement 2 | 6.3 cm |
| Measurement 3 | 6.3 cm |
| Measurement 4 | 6.1 cm |
| Measurement 5 | 6.2 cm |
| Measurement 6 | 6.1 cm |
| Measurement 7 | 6.3 cm |
| Measurement 8 | 6.0 cm |
| Measurement 9 | 6.2 cm |
| Measurement 10 | 6.4 cm |

The measurements are all close; but what is the true measurement of the line? Carl wrote a formula that takes all ten measurements (or however many measurements there are) and optimizes, or calculates, a "true" answer. The formula considers the number of measurements, the amount of the error, and carefully sorts it all out to give the optimal (or most likely) "true" measurement.

Today, more than two hundred years later, variations of the Method of Least Squares are used in all areas of math and science, and in any field that requires multiple measurements. Astronomers measuring the paths of objects in the sky use it to calculate orbits, statisticians measuring errors use it to calculate answers, and geographers measuring the curvature of the earth use it to find the best-fit line for a curve.

Adrien-Marie Legendre was the first person to formally publish the Method of Least Squares. *(Courtesy of Classic Image/Alamy)*

# three
# A Surge of Ideas

**G**auss learned much about ancient and modern languages and the history of mathematics during his years at the Collegium Carolinum, but it wasn't until he entered the University of Göttingen in 1795 that he enjoyed near-absolute freedom to explore modern math.

The University of Göttingen was located about sixty-five miles south of Brunswick, in the state of Hanover. The duke wanted Gauss to stay in Brunswick and attend the local University of Helmstedt, but Helmstedt was an older school that focused on law and religion, rather than science and math. Gauss felt that Göttingen was the better choice, and the duke continued to support him in his education despite his disapproval of the move.

At the time, the University of Göttingen was one of three universities in Germany. Wealthy students from royal families came from all parts of Europe to attend.

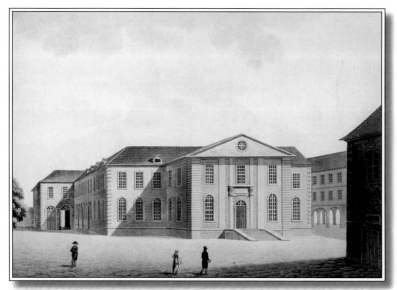

The library at the University of Göttingen in 1800.

The learning environment at the university allowed Gauss to pursue his own particular passions and attend only the lectures he considered worthy of his time. Officially, he had been admitted as a mathematics student, but he remained undecided about whether to become a mathematician or philologist. Books borrowed from the university library included a range of interests, such as travel to the Holy Land and the Cape of Good Hope; he also read novels as well as books on astronomy and opera.

Gauss was critical of certain lecturing professors at the university, and soon became known for his sometimes harsh opinions on their knowledge and teaching abilities.

One math professor in particular, Abraham G. Kästner, was a frequent target. Kästner was already advanced in age by the time Gauss arrived at the university. Nevertheless, he was busy writing the first-ever complete history of mathematics, and he is best known for writing textbooks and compiling encyclope-dias, rather than original mathematical research. Gauss once described Kästner as "the leading mathematician among poets and leading poet among mathematicians." On another occasion he drew a cartoonlike line sketch of Kästner lecturing at the blackboard—all of his calculations are wrong.

During his years at Göttingen, Gauss had few close friends. One was Johann Joseph Anton Ide, also from Brunswick. Ide was from a lower-class family, like Gauss, and had attended a simple, orphanage school. Also like Gauss, Ide's teachers had detected a special intelligence in the boy at a young age, particularly in math. With their help Ide eventually met the duke, who paid for Ide to attend the university about half a year after Gauss arrived. Ide would become a professor of mathematics at the University of Moscow.

Gauss met Farkas Wolfgang Bolyai while attending the University of Göttingen, and the two became lifelong friends.

Farkas (Wolfgang) Bolyai was perhaps Gauss's closest friend in Göttingen. Bolyai came from a family of Hungarian nobles in Transylvania. He was two years older than Gauss and had enrolled in Göttingen in 1796 as a philosophy student. Quiet, introspective, and good at mental arithmetic, Bolyai would remain friends with Gauss until the end of their lives, exchanging letters to each other for more than fifty years. Gauss once said that Bolyai was the only person who could understand his views on the foundations of mathematics.

For his part, Bolyai described Gauss as "very modest. . . . for years one could be with him without recognizing his greatness." Each swore to the other "brotherhood and the banner of truth."

Gauss kept most of his ideas and thoughts compiled in a small, bound notebook. He called the notebook *Notizenjournal* ("Diary of Notes"), and it contained nineteen, five by eight inch pages, on which were 146 entries on analysis, algebra, number theory, the law of quadratic reciprocity, the movement of comets and planets, and more.

In one diary entry, Gauss explained his thinking on how to draw a seventeen-sided polygon using a simple compass and ruler:

> Through deep reflection upon the arithmetical relations between the roots [of the equations $(xP-1)/(x-1) = 0$] during a vacation in [Brunswick], on the morning of the day in question (before I had gotten out of bed), I managed to see the desired relationship with such great clarity that I could immediately carry through the special application to the 17-gon and confirm it with a numerical calculation.

Gauss was so proud of the discovery that he published an announcement in the German journal *Allgemeine Literaturzeitung*. His old friend and professor, Eberhard A. W. Zimmermann, added a note at the end of the announcement, which read: "It deserves mentioning, that Mr. Gauss is now in his 18th year, and devoted himself here in Brunswick with equal success to philosophy and classical literature as well as higher mathematics."

# The Seventeen-sided Polygon

A 17-sided polygon is called a heptadecagon. The shape looks mysteriously like a circle at first glance. But take a closer look, and you will see 17 lines joined end to end; each forming a 152.82-degree angle.

A heptadecagon

Because 17 is a large prime number, evenly divisible only by 1, its construction with a simple compass and ruler created a special challenge for the ancient mathematicians. But Gauss figured out how to draw an exact heptadecagon using a compass and ruler in sixty-four precise, methodical steps that he explained for others to emulate. Gauss further proved why it worked mathematically.

The concluding equation of Gauss's proof looks like this:

$$\cos\frac{2\pi}{17} = \frac{\sqrt{17}-1+\sqrt{2}\sqrt{34+6\sqrt{17}}+\sqrt{2}\left(\sqrt{17}-1\right)\sqrt{17-\sqrt{17}}-8\sqrt{2}\sqrt{17+\sqrt{17}}+\sqrt{2}\sqrt{17-\sqrt{17}}}{16}$$

The part of the equation that shows cos(2Π/17) is most important. "2Π" is another way to express a complete circle, or 360 degrees. Dividing it evenly by 17 is the goal Gauss set out to achieve. The cosine is a property of the angle, and if you know the cosine of an angle, you will know that angle. Gauss showed that cos(2Π/17) could be expressed using only basic arithmetic and square roots ($\sqrt{\ }$). The square root of something is a number that can be multiplied by itself to get the original number. For example, the square root of nine is three ($\sqrt{9} = 3$) because 3 multiplied by itself (3 x 3) is nine. Looking at Gauss's concluding equation, everything on the right side of the equal sign is pure numbers and square roots. And although this is a long string of numbers, it is mathematically pretty simple (to a mathematician). This is the key point. Previous mathematicians proved that anything expressible in numbers and square roots can be constructed with a simple compass and ruler. Gauss reduced the equation to numbers and square roots, thereby making the 17-side polygon constructible. Later mathematicians would successfully construct the heptadecagon using as few as fifty steps.

Gauss's diary also revealed that that he thought some of the basic assumptions of classical geometry were wrong. Any statement suggesting a major error in classical geometry was a huge and potentially controversial claim, because it would contradict Euclid, the Greek mathematician and philosopher who lived in 300 BCE and established many of the basic rules of classical geometry.

In particular, Gauss examined parallel lines. Parallel lines are lines that stretch in both directions on a plane (a never-ending, flat surface) without ever touching. But if that surface is curved, the rules about parallel lines change.

What Gauss was hinting at became known as non-Euclidean geometry, years later; in non-Euclidean geometry, the surface is not flat, but rather concave (like the inner surface of a bowl) or convex (like the outer surface of a bowl). Here, parallel lines cannot exist. On a curved surface the lines will eventually touch each other given a limitless amount of space. Later in life, Gauss would expand on these ideas when he developed and published his Theory of Curved Surfaces. But he would remain timid about openly contradicting Euclid's geometry. "I shall probably not come to publishing my very extended investigations for a long time, and perhaps this shall never occur during my lifetime, as I am fearful of the screeching of the Boetians, were I fully to speak of my views." (Boeotia was a province of ancient Greece, northwest of Athens, whose inhabitants were considered dull and ignorant.)

After three years at the University of Göttingen, Gauss left, without a degree. He returned to Brunswick homeless, unemployed, and uncertain of his "future fate," but with a notebook full of new mathematical ideas.

# Mathematical Proofs

At Göttingen, Gauss had a surge of ideas and began writing dozens of mathematical proofs that he would perfect and publish over the next twenty-five years of his life. A proof is a demonstration that, given some assumptions (called axioms), a statement is necessarily true. Proofs can be direct or indirect, mathematical or verbal. Consider a simple verbal proof that looks like this:

> If there is fire, then there is oxygen.
> There is no oxygen here.
> Therefore, there is no fire here.

The first line is the premise: If there is fire, then there is oxygen. It is an assumption, in this case based on a fundamental fact of chemistry, that fire requires oxygen to burn. The second line states there is no oxygen here; and as a result, the last line concludes that there is no fire here. The first two lines are proof that the last line is a true statement.

You can use a similar logic to prove a mathematical statement is true—but the arguments are often written with mathematical equations rather than in words. Such proofs can get complicated very quickly. Consider a simple mathematical proof (this one with some words for clarity) that looks like this:

> The sum of two even numbers is always even.
> Consider even numbers $x$ and $y$.

Make x=2a and y=2b
Then x + y = 2a + 2b = 2(a+b)

Like the verbal proof, the first line is the premise: "The sum of two even numbers is always even," but the following lines prove this statement using math. The second line assigns letters to two even numbers, $x$ and $y$. The third line reshapes these variables, giving them each a factor of 2: $2a$ and $2b$ (the same as $x$ and $y$, but written with different symbols). This reshaping works because all even numbers are multiples of 2. Then the last line shows that $x + y = 2(a + b)$. The "2" in front of even numbers $(a + b)$ assures the sum of the two will always be even because anything you multiply by 2 will result in an even number. In this case, the last line proves that the premise is true.

Gauss wrote dozens of complicated mathematical proofs; they were his own, original solutions to mathematical problems. He was always searching for the most basic truths in mathematics, and he believed that the study of mathematics was the best way to educate the human mind. While working out a proof, Gauss rarely shared details about his work with his friends or teachers. He preferred to work and think alone. Perhaps as a result, Gauss maintained only a couple close friends during his three years at Göttingen.

# four
# Exploring Astronomy

**B**ack in Brunswick, Gauss began the arduous task of finding a way to finance his mathematical pursuits. At first, things looked bleak. In a letter dated November 19, 1798, Gauss revealed to his close friend Bolyai that he was, "living for the most part now on credit because my financial prospects are all shattered." But assistance soon arrived thanks to Zimmermann, who asked Duke Carl Wilhelm Ferdinand to continue his financial support of Gauss. The duke agreed.

In a follow-up letter to Bolyai, Gauss reported "he has explained that I am to continue receiving the sum which I enjoyed in Göttingen (which amounts to 158 thalers annually and is now fairly adequate to my needs)."

The duke asked for one thing in return for his patronage, however. "He desires further that I become a doctor

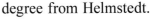

of philosophy," Gauss told Bolyai, "but I am going to post-pone it until my *Work* is done, when I hope I can become one without costs and without the usual harlequinery."

For the next year, Gauss seems to have split his time between Brunswick and the town of Helmstedt, about thirty miles to the east. The University of Helmstedt was there, and it was home to a fine university library, a great resource for Gauss in his work.

Gauss met Johann Friedrich Pfaff, a math professor at the University of Helmstedt, and the two became great admirers of each other. Gauss described Pfaff as "an excellent geom-eter as well as a good man and my warm friend; a man of innocent, childlike character, without any of the violent emo-tions which so dishonor a man and are widespread among scholars."

Gauss lived in a room in Pfaff's home, which he furnished himself, and among the math problems he was working on during this time was his final paper to earn his doctorate degree from Helmstedt.

In early 1799 Gauss com-pleted his thesis—a proof of the fundamental theorem of algebra—and on July 16, 1799, he received his doc-toral degree, without being required to appear for an oral examination. The duke

Gauss became good friends with Johann Friedrich Pfaff and described him as "an excellent geometer."

 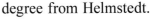

A building of the former University of Helmstedt *(Courtesy of Werner Otto/Alamy)*

## Fundamental Theorem of Algebra

The Fundamental Theorem of Algebra says that for a certain type of equation, the number of solutions is always equal to the highest exponent, or power, of the variable in that equation.

This applies to equations that have only one variable, such as $x + 3 = 6$. In this case, the $x$ is raised to the power of 1 (it's actually $x^1$, we just don't write the number one as an exponent). According to the theorem, because the highest exponent is one, this equation has only one solution ($x = 3$). In the case of $x^2 - 3x = -2$, the highest exponent is two. So this equation has two solutions ($x = 1$ and 2).

Today, experts suggest the Fundamental Theorem of Algebra is misnamed. It is not only about algebra, but about analyzing equations. In the greater field of mathematics the theorem is important because it assures an equation has a set amount of solutions.

paid to have his protégé's thesis published, and Gauss, in turn, dedicated the work to Duke Ferdinand:

I account it the highest joy, most gracious Prince, that you allow me to grace with your exalted name this work which I offer to you in fulfillment of the holy obligations of loyal love. For if your Grace had not opened up for me the access to sciences, if your unremitting benefactions had not encouraged my studies up to this day, I would never have been able to dedicate myself completely to the mathematical sciences to which I am inclined by nature.

Ceres (lower left) in comparison to the sizes of Earth and the moon.
*(Courtesy of NASA)*

In the years following Gauss's doctorate work on the fundamental theorem of algebra he started to move away from pure math. Instead of only fundamental proofs and theorems he began to think about more practical math applications, including calculating the orbits of planets.

At the time, astronomers across Europe were attempting to locate the minor planet Ceres. An Italian astronomer, Giuseppe Piazzi of the Palermo Observatory, had discovered the planet on January 1, 1801, and named it for the Roman goddess of agriculture. Gauss's interest intensified after reading an article published in the German astronomical periodical called *Monatliche Correspondenz (Monthly Correspondence)*. The editor of the periodical, Franz Xavier von Zach, was also director of an observatory in Seeberg near Goth. In the article, von Zach listed Piazzi's observed locations. Unfortunately, Piazzi only saw the planet he called Ceres for forty days before it disappeared behind the sun. Each time he saw the planet, he marked its exact location on a map of the sky. These twenty-four observed locations gave him, and others, only a glimpse at Ceres's complete orbit. Piazzi had seen Ceres for only 9° of its 360° elliptical path around the sun.

Italian astronomer Giuseppe Piazzi discovered the minor planet Ceres in 1801.

Using this 9° of observation information, many astronomers were working to calculate the exact orbit of the new planet. If the orbit was calculated correctly, then astronomers would be able to predict when and where Ceres would appear in the night sky again.

Calculating the shape of the orbit from such a small number of observations was clearly a mathematical problem, and Gauss was drawn into the challenge. Most astronomers working on the problem were creating elliptical orbits and trying to fit the observed locations to the orbits. Gauss, instead, used the observed locations to construct the orbit, and by November, he had solved the problem.

Gauss sent his orbit predictions to many astronomers. At the same time, the *Monatliche Correspondenz* published Gauss's calculations and publicized his prediction on when and where Ceres would appear again in the night sky. When the small planet was rediscovered in December 1801, it appeared almost exactly where Gauss had predicted.

Gauss achieved international fame when his calculations helped predict the position of Ceres. In 1809 he explained his calculations in the *Theory of the Motion of the Heavenly Bodies Revolving round the Sun in Conic Sections.* Later, those calculations became known as the Gauss-Jordan elimination and the Method of Least Squares. Gauss-Jordan elimination is an algorithm for solving systems of linear equations; to determine Ceres's orbit, Gauss solved a system of seventeen linear equations.

Gauss's unexpected achievement in astronomy captured the attention of the czar of Russia, who asked Gauss to become

director of the observatory at Petrograd Academy, in St. Petersburg. Such a position would have meant a secure salary for twenty-five-year-old Gauss, something he had never had before. But it would have also meant leaving

A 1828 portrait of Gauss

Germany, and Gauss was deeply loyal to the duke, whose financial support had made it possible for him to attend school and then university.

When the duke heard of the Russian czar's offer, he stepped in to keep Gauss in Germany, raising his stipend from 158 to 400 thalers per year. Gauss accepted the money, turned down the job, and continued his work in Germany.

## Calculating the Orbit of Ceres

Calculating the orbit of a planet based on a few observations is a purely mathematical problem. The orbit is in the shape of an ellipse, and the observations are points along that ellipse.

Accuracy is the key to this calculation. Given a certain number of points along the ellipse, there can be many different ellipses that fit those points. Each ellipse is a possible, approximate solution to the problem. But the astronomers attempting to calculate the orbit of Ceres weren't after just any elliptical orbit to fit the observation points, they were looking for the best-fit, true orbit based on a small set of observed locations.

To calculate the best-fit ellipse, and therefore the most likely "true" orbit of the planet Ceres, Gauss used a two-step approach. First, he determined multiple, approximate orbits that fit the observed locations using any mathematical method that worked. In some cases, he used the approximate orbits determined by other astronomers. Second, he applied his Method of Least Squares that he developed in college to eliminate errors in these approximations. The Method allowed Gauss to combine all the possible elliptical orbit approximations, minimize the errors in these approximations, and determine the most likely "true" orbit. It worked.

The Royal Astronomical Society of London honored Gauss with a lengthy obituary after his death in 1855. Among the many achievements noted was his work to calculate the proper orbit of celestial bodies: "The *Theoria Motus* [Theory of Motion] will always be classed among those great works, the appearance of which forms an epoch in the history of science."

# five
# Year of Turmoil

The same year that Gauss calculated the orbit of Ceres, he also published one of the most significant works of his lifetime. The *Disquisitiones Arithmeticae* (*Discourses on Number Theory*) was a textbook that brought the work of many different mathematicians together in one place. Before the publication of *Disquisitiones*, number theory was a consortium of disconnected theorems and ideas from many different minds. Gauss corrected errors in other theorems and wrote new proofs to essentially connect the dots between ideas. It included Gauss's original work from previous years, and established a format for future math texts. Ultimately, *Disquisitiones* not only unified a specific field of mathematics, it created entire new avenues to pursue.

The great Italian mathematician Joseph-Louis Lagrange wrote Gauss shortly after the publication to express his praise: "Your *Disquisitiones* have with one stroke elevated you to

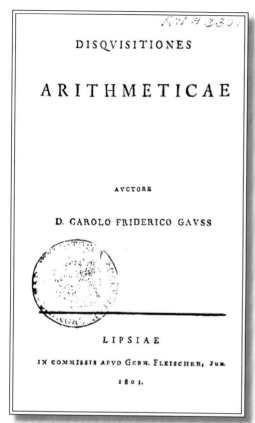

DISQVISITIONES

ARITHMETICAE

AVCTORE

D. CAROLO FRIDERICO GAVSS

LIPSIAE

IN COMMISSIS APVD GERH. FLEISCHER, JUN.

1801.

The title page of the first edition of *Disquisitiones Arithmeticae*

the rank of the foremost mathematicians, and the contents of the last section [theory of the equations of circle division] I look on as the most beautiful discovery which has been made for a long time."

Aside from the mathematical content of the text-book, Gauss established a format with *Disquisitiones* that became the standard among scholars. Gauss began each section of the book by explaining a theorem that mathematics sought to prove. Next he provided the proof and followed this with a list of corollaries. In math, a corollary is an idea that follows logically, with little or no proof, from a statement that has already been proven. Such corollaries often provide new ideas for future study.

In the *Disquisitiones*, for example, Gauss explains the Law of Quadratic Reciprocity, and then proves it mathematically. The Law of Quadratic Reciprocity is one of the great theorems of classical numbers theory and was established by other mathematicians shortly before Gauss was born. However, the first complete proof of this law was given by Gauss in 1796, when he was nineteen. This proof established Gauss as one of the best mathematicians of the time.

## The Law of Quadratic Reciprocity

The premise of the Law of Quadratic Reciprocity is that one can determine the solvability of two sets of equations using a specific method. In this case, "solvability" means the chances that one can determine the value of a variable in the equations (such as an "$x$"), and the "equations" take a very specific form.

The Law of Quadratic Reciprocity involves what is known as quadratic equations. These always take the form: $ax^2 + bx + c = 0$, where $x$ is the unknown variable and $a$ and $b$ are regular numbers. The Law says that given two quadratic equations, one should be able to determine the chances of finding the value of the $x$ variable. It doesn't tell you *how* to find the value of $x$, it only tells you your *chances* of finding that value.

Gauss's proof of the Law of Quadratic Reciprocity was only a small part of the *Disquisitiones*. The first three sections include a review of previous theorems and results from other mathematicians, while the remaining sections include more of Gauss's original work. The *Disquisitiones* was one of the last mathematics textbooks to be written and published in Latin. It wasn't fully translated into English until nearly two hundred years later, in 1965; though the ideas made

— 133 —

formae $4n + 1$, per $b$, $b'$, $b''$ etc. numeros pri-
mos formae $4n + 3$ denotabimus; per $A$, $A'$,
$A''$ etc. numeros quoscunque formae $4n + 1$, per
$B$, $B'$, $B''$ etc. autem numeros quoscunque formae $4n + 3$; tandem litera $R$ duabus quanti-
tatibus interposita indicabit, priorem sequentis
esse residuum, sicuti litera $N$ significationem
contrariam habebit. Ex. gr. $+ 5 R 11$, $\pm 2 N 5$,
indicabit $+ 5$ ipsius $11$ esse residuum, $+ 2$ vel
$- 2$ esse ipsius $5$ non-residuum. Iam collato
theoremate fundamentali cum theorematibus
art. 111, sequentes propositiones facile dedu-
centur.

| Si | erit |
|---|---|
| 1. $\pm a R a'$ ........ | $\pm a' R a$ |
| 2. $\pm a N a'$ ........ | $\pm a' N a$ |
| 3. $\begin{bmatrix} + & a R b \\ - & a N b \end{bmatrix}$ ....... | $\pm b R a$ |
| 4. $\begin{bmatrix} + & a N b \\ - & a R b \end{bmatrix}$ ....... | $\pm b N a$ |
| 5. $\pm b R a$ ........ | $\begin{bmatrix} + & a R b \\ - & a N b \end{bmatrix}$ |
| 6. $\pm b N a$ ........ | $\begin{bmatrix} + & a N b \\ - & a R b \end{bmatrix}$ |
| 7. $\begin{bmatrix} + & b R b' \\ - & b N b' \end{bmatrix}$ ...... | $\begin{bmatrix} + & b' N b \\ - & b' R b \end{bmatrix}$ |
| 8. $\begin{bmatrix} + & b N b' \\ - & b R b' \end{bmatrix}$ ...... | $\begin{bmatrix} + & b' R b \\ - & b' N a \end{bmatrix}$ |

I 3

The proof of the Law of
Quadratic Reciprocity
on a page from Gauss's
*Disquisitiones Arithmeticae.*

their way into schol-
arly research fields long
before then.

By 1802 Gauss was
again drawn back into
astronomy. A physician
and experienced astron-
omer named Wilhelm
Olbers had just discov-
ered the minor planet
Pallas. When Gauss
read of this rediscovery
he wrote to Olbers in his
hometown in Bremen,
Germany, to request his
new observed locations of the planet. Gauss wanted the new
data points to perfect his orbit calculations, but he soon became
friends with the senior scientist.

The friendship was mutually beneficial. Olbers was an
established astronomer who had completed his work at the
University of Göttingen twenty years before Gauss. He knew
many important people in the field and would work behind the
scenes on Gauss's behalf on many occasions in the future.

## "New Proofs for Known Truths"

During his life, Gauss published only about half of his mathematical and scientific discoveries. Historians have long speculated on the reasons why: too many ideas, not enough time; withholding information to avoid criticism; little or no regard for recognitions or honor; even being a slow writer, something Gauss himself admitted. In March 1817 Gauss reviewed one of his seven proofs of the Law of Quadratic Reciprocity in a German journal, and perhaps a clue can be found in what he wrote:

> It is characteristic of higher arithmetic that many of its most beautiful theorems can be discovered by induction with the greatest of ease but have proofs that lie anywhere but near at hand and are often found only after many fruitless investigations with the aid of deep analysis and lucky combinations. This significant phenomenon arises from the wonderful concatenation of different teachings of this branch of mathematics, and from this it often happens that many theorems, whose proof for years was sought in vain, are later proved in many different ways. As soon as a new result is discovered by induction, one must consider as the first requirement the finding of a proof by *any possible* means. But after such good fortune, one must not in higher arithmetic consider the investigation closed or view the search for other proofs as a superfluous luxury. For sometimes one does not at first come upon the most beautiful

> and simplest proof, and then it is just the insight
> into the wonderful concatenation of truth in higher
> arithmetic that is the chief attraction for study
> and often leads to the discovery of new truths.
> For these reasons the finding of new proofs for
> known truths is often at least as important as the
> discovery itself.

Gauss reciprocated by helping Olbers with his work in astronomy. In March of 1802 Olbers discovered what appeared to be a new planet, and he asked Gauss to help him calculate the orbit. Before Gauss's orbital calculating technique, such an accomplishment may have taken years to refine. But twenty days after Olbers' first sighting of the new planet, Gauss had calculated the orbit, claiming his achievement was only a confirmation of Newton's laws of gravity. The friendship between Gauss and Olbers continued, primarily through letters, though Gauss would travel the two hundred miles north to Bremen to visit Olbers many times.

Gauss continued his work and maintained his friendships for the next few years. But in 1803, he turned his attention to a new interest, his future wife. In a letter to his friend Bolyai, Gauss described his new relationship with Johanna Osthoff, the only child of a tanner.

> Since my last letter to you I have made a lot of new acquaintances.
> . . . The most beautiful, however, is the friendship of a splendid
> girl, exactly such a girl as I have always desired for a life
> companion. A wondrously fair Madonna countenance, a mirror
> of spiritual peace and health, kind, somewhat romantic eyes, a
> perfect figure and size (that is something), a clear understanding

Wilhelm Olbers *(Courtesy of The Print Collector/Alamy)*

and an intelligent conversation (that is also something), but a quiet, happy, modest, and chaste angelic soul which can harm no one, that is the best.

As for Gauss, he was blond, with blue eyes and thick eyebrows. He stood about five feet two inches tall, was rather stocky, and walked with a measured gait. He was nearsighted, and sometimes wore glasses. In later years, when his hair had turned silvery gray, Gauss seldom was seen without his trademark black velvet cap.

Gauss enjoyed an occasional glass of wine, smoked a pipe, played chess and whist, and he was considered quiet and mild-mannered, yet also austere and conservative, especially with his praise of others.

Gauss on a German stamp

A year after meeting Johanna, Gauss proposed, and they were married on October 9, 1805. They rented a small apartment above a shop on one of the main streets in Brunswick and lived on the duke's four hundred thalers per year payment to Gauss. In 1806, their first son was born; they named him Josef after the discoverer of the planet Ceres, Giuseppe Piazzi (Giuseppe is Italian for Josef). That same year the duke raised Gauss's yearly salary to six hundred thalers, an impressive sum at the time.

Life seemed to be falling into place for Gauss, until suddenly everything began to change.

## six

# Changing Direction

The French Revolution had begun in 1789, when Gauss was twelve, and after a decade of social and political turmoil an unknown French general, Napoleon Bonaparte, had emerged as dictator. On December 2, 1804, Bonaparte crowned himself emperor of France; less than a week later, a coalition of countries (Britain, Austria, Russia, the Netherlands, Sweden, Naples, and a collection of German principalities) formed an alliance against France, with the intent of forcing France back inside its borders. Bonaparte was not to be stopped, however; his French army defeated coalition forces in battle after battle. Once French troops came dangerously near to Brunswick, but the French emperor was asked to spare the town because, "the foremost mathematician of his time lives there."

By 1806 Prussia had joined the coalition, and King Frederick William III of Prussia made Duke Ferdinand

Napoleon Bonaparte *(Courtesy of The Print Collector/Alamy)*

commander of the Prussian forces. A nephew and pupil of Frederick the Great, the duke had enjoyed a long and celebrated military career, but now he was seventy-one years old and commanding an army of men who were no match for Bonaparte's well-trained and disciplined force. The duke was mortally wounded by a musket ball at the Battle of Jena, and Brunswick lost its independence. Bonaparte refused a request to allow the duke to die in Brunswick, among his

Napoleon rallies his troops a the Battle of Jena. It was during this battle that Gauss's benefactor, Duke Ferdinand, was mortally wounded with a musket ball. *(Courtesy of IMAGNO/Austrian Archives/Getty Images)*

friends and people. Gauss often told the story of the morning of October 25, 1806, when a horse-drawn carriage carrying the dying duke left for Altona. Gauss witnessed the departure from a window at his house, which was located opposite the castle gate. The duke, who had intended to flee, died on November 10, 1806, after several days of travel, in a hovel outside of Altona.

Gauss was grief-stricken. For fourteen years Duke Ferdinand had made it possible for him to study and work independently, by providing him with a stipend. Now Gauss's future was in jeopardy. Gauss opposed Napoleon and hated that his native state had fallen under French control. He considered taking his family to England, but then decided against such a move.

During this period of social and political turmoil, Gauss had started exchanging letters about number-theory problems with a French mathematician by the name of M. LeBlanc. He even mentioned LeBlanc to his friend Olbers in a letter: "Recently I had the pleasure to receive a letter from LeBlanc, a young geometer in Paris, who made himself enthusiastically familiar with higher mathematics and showed how deeply he penetrated into my Disqu. Arithm. . . ."

One day in late fall of 1806, a French officer visited Gauss at his home to ask about his health and then offer him protection, if needed. This offer had been sent at the request of Mademoiselle Sophie Germain in Paris. Gauss told the officer that he didn't know anyone in Paris named Germain. But three months later, he learned that LeBlanc was in fact Sophie Germain.

Germain, who was a year older than Gauss and a member of a wealthy Parisian family, had concealed her identity

A bust of French mathematician Sophie Germain (*Courteesy of Getty Images*)

because she feared that Gauss would not have taken her seriously if he had known that she was a woman. Most women of that era received little if any education. Germain was the exception; she was a self-taught and highly accomplished mathematician. She needed to discuss her ideas, and Gauss was the greatest number theorist of that time. When Gauss learned that Germain was a woman, he wrote to her:

> How can I describe my astonishment and admiration on seeing my esteemed correspondent M. LeBlanc metamorphosed into this celebrated person, yielding a copy so brilliant it is hard to believe? The taste for the abstract sciences in general and, above all, for the mysteries of numbers, is very rare: this is not surprising, since the charms of this sublime science in all their beauty reveal themselves only to those who have the courage to fathom them. But when a woman, because of her sex, our customs and prejudices, encounters infinitely more obstacles than men in familiarizing herself with their knotty problems, yet overcomes these fetters and penetrates that which is most hidden, she doubtless has the most noble courage, extraordinary talent, and superior genius.

Gauss recommended that the University of Göttingen grant Germain an honorary degree, but she died of cancer in 1831 before the degree could be awarded.

Meanwhile, unbeknownst to Gauss, his friend Olbers had been working to secure Gauss a position as director of the astronomical observatory at the University of Göttingen. In a letter to a professor at Göttingen, who was also an advisor to the government, he wrote:

> This young man of 25 years is the first of his mathematical contemporaries. I believe I am quite a competent judge because not only have I read his works, but I have also been his trusted

correspondent. . . . His knowledge, his extraordinary dexterity in the analytical and astronomical calculus, his indefatigable activity and industriousness, his uncomparable genius aroused my highest admiration which has been ever increasing, the more of his ideas he has been communicating to me in our correspondence. He loves astronomy enthusiastically. . . . He desires to be an astronomer at some observatory.

After much discussion with Olbers, Gauss eventually decided to accept the position. The family moved to the university town later that year, in 1807, and moved into an apartment only a few steps from the old observatory in Göttingen. After the Napoleonic wars, Göttingen had been incorporated into the new French kingdom of Westphalia, but none of these political developments hampered Gauss's work.

Gauss on the terrace of the Göttingen Observatory *(Courtesy of Photo Researchers/Alamy)*

Gauss's new job included teaching classes at the university as well as maintaining the observatory. Teaching did not appeal to him; he considered it an intrusion on his own research time. "For a professor of mathematics it consists of eternal work to just teach the ABC's of his science;" he wrote in a letter to Olbers, "most of the few students who continue only gather a pile of information and become half-educated, for the rare gifted students will not allow themselves to be educated through lectures but instead learn by themselves. And through this thankless work the professor loses his precious time."

Living close to the observatory, however, seemed to more than make up for the burdens of teaching. In letters to friends, Johanna said that Gauss often didn't come to bed until after one o'clock in the morning because he was making new observations of the night sky.

## Gauss's Students

Although Gauss professed an aversion to teaching, he was admired by and made a marked impression on his students, several of whom would go on to become influential mathematicians in their own right. When he lectured, his students sat around a table covered with books, and he sat in an armchair at one of the end of the table. J. W. Richard Dedekind was Gauss's last doctoral student, and he would go on to do important work in abstract algebra, algebraic number theory, and the foundations of real numbers. Fifty years after

Dedekind heard Gauss give a lecture on the method of least squares, he still recalled the beauty of it:

> Usually he sat in a comfortable attitude, looking down, slightly stooped, with hands folded above his lap. He spoke freely, very clearly, simply and right to the point; but when he wanted to emphasize a new viewpoint, in which he used an especially characteristic word, the he suddenly lifted his head, turn to one of those sitting next to him, and gazed at him with his beautiful, penetrating blue eyes during the emphatic speech. . . . If he proceeded from an explanation of principles to the development of mathematical formulas, then he got up, and in a stately very upright posture he wrote on a blackboard beside him in his peculiarly beautiful handwriting: he always succeeded through economy and deliberate arrangement in making do with a rather small space. For numerical examples, on whose careful completion he placed special value, he brought along the requisite data on little slips of paper.

With the observatory there for his use as a research tool, Gauss wrote a book summarizing his work in astronomy called *Theoria Motus (Theory of Motion)*. Published in 1809, Gauss describes his methods of observation including calculating the different shapes of orbits (elliptical, circular, and parabolic). The book would become a textbook for professional astronomers in coming decades.

Gauss flourished in his career, and he enjoyed stability at home as well. Johanna successfully gave birth to their second child, a daughter called Wilhelmine (Minna) in 1808.

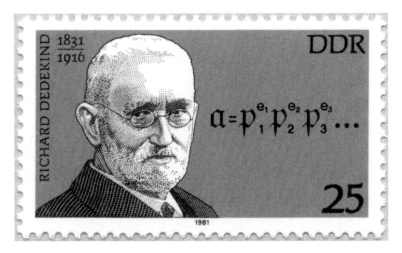

$$a = p_1^{e_1} p_2^{e_2} p_3^{e_3} \dots$$

J. W. Richard Dedekind

Like their first child Josef, Minna was named after one of Gauss's colleagues: in this case, his good friend Wilhelm Olbers. In a letter to his friend Bolyai, Gauss shared his joy: "The days fly happily by in home life's daily course; when our daughter gets a new tooth or our son learns a couple of new words, it is almost as important as when a new star or a new truth is discovered."

In 1809 Johanna gave birth to their third child, a son named Louis for the astronomer Carl Ludwig Harding, the discoverer of a planet whose orbit Gauss had calculated. The labor was difficult, however, and mother and baby did not recover. Johanna died within a month of giving birth. The loss of his wife devastated Gauss, and he asked Olbers if he could stay with him for a few weeks, "to gather new strength in the arms of your friendship—strength for a life which is only valuable because it belongs to my three small children." Within a few months the mathematician would suffer another devastating loss when Louis died.

Gauss's second wife, Minna

Gauss searched to fill Johanna's role in the home. Within a year of her death, he had married her best friend, Friedrica Wilhelmine Waldeck (who, like his oldest daughter, went by the nickname Minna). Minna was the daughter of a professor and from a more privileged background than Gauss. In a proposal letter to her, Gauss spoke of his "throbbing heart because my life's happiness depends on it," and he asked her not to judge him too harshly because his proposal came "barely a year after losing such a beloved wife."

My dearest, I do not want to bribe you into the most important decision of your life. I honor you too much to wish to conceal that I can offer you only a divided heart from which the image of the glorious shadow will never disappear. But if you knew how the departed loved and esteemed you, you would understand that—in this important moment while I ask you to decide whether you can step into her place—I see the beloved departed vividly, acknowledging cheerfully my wishes and wishing me and our children happiness and bliss.

Minna was very different from Johanna. Instead of being innately cheerful and easy-going, Minna was at times depressed and quiet. Nevertheless, Gauss and Minna had three children within five years. Their sons Eugene and Wilhelm were born in 1811 and 1813, respectively, while their daughter Therese was born in 1816.

# seven
# Mapping the Earth

After the birth of his last child, Gauss turned his attention to a new pursuit: mapping the earth. His involvement began in late 1816 when Heinrich Christian Schumacher, one of his first students at Göttingen, wrote to Gauss and asked for help mapping the kingdom of Denmark. At the time, many of the major countries in Europe were mapping their lands—a time consuming and tedious process. Accurate maps showing the shape of the land were difficult to come by and mapping instruments were rudimentary.

Gauss's careful and thorough nature seems to have been a good match for the mapping work. After the mapping of Denmark was completed, Schumacher hired Gauss to map the kingdom of Hanover, a small German state about the size of Manhattan Island in the United States. Gauss directed the

Hanover mapping project nearly from start to finish, a task that took more than twenty years to complete.

Gauss and his team of mapmakers would measure an area of land by laying out an imaginary grid of triangles connected at the sides. Today, this method is known as triangulation. Triangulation begins with a team at one point on the land. Team members then select two distant points (sometimes up to twenty miles away) that can be seen with the human eye. Once the location of these points is determined, the length of one side of the imaginary triangle can be calculated. This length can then be used to determine the angles of the triangle and obtain an area of the land inside the shape. By creating

Heinrich Christian Schumacher wrote to Gauss in 1816 and asked for help mapping the kingdom of Denmark.

a grid of known triangles over the land a fairly precise map can be constructed.

During this work, Gauss invented a new mapping instrument to help determine the points of the imaginary triangles. His instrument, called the heliotrope, used a small mirror to reflect sunlight over a great distance. Though use of the heliotrope was restricted to sunny days, it soon became a standard in mapping work. Gauss invented the heliotrope (*helio* meaning sun and *trope* meaning turn) in 1821.

Because of the sun (and the warmer temperatures), summer was the time for mapping the land. For eight or nine

A diagram of Gauss's heliotrope

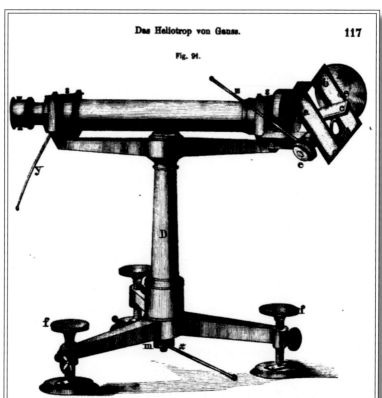

summers in a row Gauss traveled through Hanover with a team of mapmakers taking measurements of the kingdom. Each measurement was taken multiple times, and Gauss applied his Method of Least Squares to determine the most likely, true measurement of the land.

Such work was not easy. Gauss was constantly traveling, looking for places to stay and negotiating with landowners for permission to work on private property. On one occasion Gauss was thrown from a horse and received cuts, bruises, and a black eye. And most days involved a lot of walking in the hot summer heat carrying heavy survey equipment. It was a big change for Gauss, who was more accustomed to sitting, reading, and thinking about problems on paper.

Gauss was still director of the astronomical observatory at the University of Göttingen, and in 1816, after nearly a decade of construction, it was finally completed. During the construction, Gauss had helped select and purchase new instruments. And partially for his benefit, the new observatory included an apartment for the Gauss family.

By this time, Minna had a housekeeper and a nurse to assist with the home and the five children. But Minna's health was not good. She was often tired, coughing, and out of breath. Over time, Minna became more and more bedridden.

Shortly after the Gauss family moved into the spacious new observatory apartment, Gauss's mother came to live with them. Gauss's father had died nine years earlier, and since his death, Dorothea had lived alone in the house where Gauss grew up. She hadn't left Brunswick for forty years, so a new town and a new home was a major change for her. But even at age seventy-four, Dorothea was in better health than Minna. She spent her days going to the local market to

A case filled with Gauss's instruments at Göttingen's Institute for Geophysics. *(Courtesy of Walter Sanders/Time Life Pictures/Getty Images)*

buy gingerbread for her grandchildren and lingering in the observatory garden. She was beginning to go blind at this time, but it didn't seem to slow her down.

Every day Gauss came home to have afternoon tea with his mother, Minna, and his daughter Therese. Gauss knew by now that the bedridden Minna was quite sick, and he seemed to cherish these family tea times.

While his wife grew weaker, Gauss continued to map the kingdom of Hanover, and slowly became interested in how a curved surface is represented on a flat map—a new mathematical problem again grounded in geometry.

By this time, different types of map projections already existed and each handled curved surfaces differently. The challenge of any map projection is to represent the two-dimensional curvature of the earth accurately on a one-dimensional piece of paper. But this is difficult to do without some distortion of the actual shapes. A Mercator projection of the earth, for example, is created by wrapping a cylinder around the globe and flattening the globe out onto the cylinder in straight lines. This results in relatively stretched out north and south poles. A stereographic projection, by contrast, is created by drawing circles through different points on the globe. In this case all the angles and relative sizes are preserved, but the entire globe cannot be easily shown on a single surface.

Gauss, not surprisingly, wanted the most accurate maps possible. He contributed to this mapping task in two unique ways. First, he calculated massive land areas from the survey points in his head; and second, he wrote a new theorem to ensure the maps' accuracy.

To calculate the land areas, Gauss used the thousands of survey points gathered by his summer field crew. In one

1875 Mercator Projection

Division of Maps
JUL 30 1948
Library of Congress

Ca 1: 130,000,000

case, Gauss had 3,000 triangulation points that he used to calculate the area of the land. Because of his unusual ability to do math in his head, he was particularly suited for this task. But it was still tedious work.

To assure himself that the measurements were accurate, Gauss wrote the Theory of Curved Surfaces, published in 1827.

## Theory of Curved Surfaces

Gauss's Theory of Curved Surfaces, also known as the "Remarkable Theorem," states, "If a curved surface is developed upon any other surface whatever, the measure of curvature in each point remains unchanged."

This may not make much sense on the first reading, or the second or third, but the theorem essentially resolves a main issue in mapping curved surfaces. A prerequisite for understanding the theory is to understand the concept of Gaussian Curvature, that a curve can be measured and quantified. A second point is that curves can be formed in more than one type of space. This theorem states that the curvature is independent of the space.

In 1827 Gauss published a small book to explain and prove this Theory of Curved Surfaces, which contains page after page of lengthy mathematical equations. In a letter to a friend Gauss wrote, "all the measurements in the world do not outweigh one theorem by which the science of eternal truths is really carried forward."

# eight
# Exploring Magnetism

**W**hen Gauss finished the survey of Hanover, he began the third and last major chapter of his professional research life. He had already made historic contributions to the fields of astronomy and mapping; now he turned his attention to magnets and electricity. As early as 1803 Gauss had written to his friend Olbers about his interest in physics, but had never devoted time to its study. Now, the opportunity presented itself.

In 1830, the head of the physics department at the University of Göttingen died and Gauss was asked for his recommendation to fill the position. He suggested a few people, but he seemed to clearly favor a twenty-seven-year-old German named Wilhelm Weber. At the time, Weber was an assistant professor at a smaller university in Germany. Gauss had heard him lecture once and openly expressed his opinion that Weber was well-organized and had promising new research ideas.

Profiles of Gauss (foreground) and Wilhelm Weber *(Courtesy of Mary Evans Picture Library/Alamy)*

The only concern was his young age and ability to handle the administrative side of the job. Nevertheless, the University of Göttingen took Gauss's advice and offered Weber the job in 1831. Weber accepted.

When Weber settled into his new position, he and Gauss began working together almost immediately. They began by studying magnetism, the idea that something can naturally attract or repel something else. This work was fundamentally grounded in math but still tied to the real world with physics. In a short time, Gauss was writing scholarly papers on his new discoveries in magnetism.

In 1833, Gauss published his first paper on the magnetism of the earth. In it he established the three measurements that determine the magnetic properties of an object: mass, length, and time. Mass is the amount of matter in an object, length is the dimension of the object, and time is a sequence of events that happens. Gauss was the first person to realize that these three things determine the magnetism of an object, and the first to show that a quantity of magnetism could be calculated with math. He also discovered that magnetism is affected by temperature, something no one at the time knew.

At the time, the study of magnetism was a relatively new field. But Gauss and Weber saw that it was becoming more and more popular and decided to help organize the new research movement. Together, they created a professional association devoted to sharing new information on magnetism. Eventually they would write more than two-thirds of the articles published in the association's professional research journal.

Like many of Gauss's professional friendships, the relationship seemed to be mutually beneficial for both scientists. Weber, who was single and lived with his sister, frequently came to dinner at Gauss's house. And Gauss went to Weber's home for long hours of conversation. Professionally, the two complemented each other. Weber knew the research field of physics and was good at constructing experiments. While older and more-established Gauss could provide university resources and theoretical insight (along with his usual calculating talents).

In 1833, Gauss's access to resources paid off when he officially asked the university to build a new laboratory dedicated to the study of magnetism. Perhaps because the request came from Gauss, the university immediately funded the project and the two scientists went to work designing the new research facility—the first of its kind anywhere in the world.

To study magnetism, which is affected by the tiniest environmental influences such as air currents, the building design is crucial. The construction materials and floor plans can affect experimental results. When the building was finally completed at the end of 1833, it became instantly popular among researchers. Other universities in Europe soon followed Göttingen's example, and more magnetics laboratories were constructed.

By now Gauss's five children were nearing adulthood and were beginning to make their own decisions, with or without their father's approval. In time, each child would choose a different path in life.

Gauss's oldest son Josef attended the university for a short time and worked closely as an assistant to his father mapping Hanover. When that project was completed, he enlisted as a soldier in the German military. Eventually Josef became chief building officer with the Hanover railway company.

Gauss's first daughter Minna, by contrast, is said to have been Gauss's clear favorite. Gauss's second wife once wrote to Gauss describing her stepdaughter, "The older she gets, the more lovable the little girl becomes, and certainly she is the crown of our children." Minna married Heinrich August von Ewald, a theology professor whom Gauss particularly liked.

The first son of his second wife, Eugene, was the most difficult (and perhaps the most intelligent) of Gauss's children. Eugene had a special talent for learning languages and solving problems. At a young age Eugene decided he wanted to study philosophy and Gauss strongly objected, apparently wanting to keep his children out of science for fear they would tarnish the Gauss name. Instead, Gauss enrolled Eugene in law school in Göttingen, where Eugene quickly took up gambling and drinking.

One evening Eugene held an elaborate dinner party for his friends and sent the bill to his father. The resulting argument ended when Eugene moved to the United States, without saying goodbye to anyone in his family, including his ailing mother. Gauss never saw Eugene again but blamed him for hastening Minna's poor health. Eventually, Eugene became a successful farmer and banker and died a very wealthy man in St. Charles, Missouri. His descendents continue to live in that area today.

Gauss's third son, Wilhelm, wanted to be a farmer and never attended university. He married in Germany and took his wife to the United States, settling near his brother Eugene in Missouri. Wilhelm bought a farm, but made his real wealth working as a shopkeeper and businessman. Like Eugene, Gauss never saw Wilhelm again.

Gauss's youngest daughter, Therese, was much like her mother, Minna: smart but often sad, and always ill in some way or another. Therese and her half-sister Minna were reportedly very different and did not always get along. Yet Therese was loyal to her father. After her mother's death Therese cared for the house and was Gauss's constant companion.

In spite of all that was happening in his personal life, Gauss's work life continued uninterrupted. During this year he and Weber invented the first working telegraph, a device that used magnets and electricity to transmit messages

Gauss's youngest daughter, Therese

over long distances. They strung a wire from the observatory where Gauss lived to the laboratory where Weber worked, a distance of about a mile and a half. When they wanted to communicate, they used magnets to send a series of electrical pulses that stood for words. (The communication code was similar to the long and short beeps of the well-known Morse code, which was invented about ten years later.) It was the first communication instrument of its kind.

## Unit of Magnetism

When Gauss established the three measurements of magnetism—mass, length, and time—he created a new scientific unit of measurement. Today that unit is called, appropriately, the gauss (G). As an inch measures the distance of a line, the gauss measures the magnetism of a specific area in space. Mathematically speaking, $1G = 1Mx/cm^2$. ("Mx" stands for a maxwell, a quantity of magnetism.) The equation says that one gauss is equal to one unit of magnetism (the Mx) across a square centimeter (a square with four, centimeter-long sides).

For the first time, magnetism could be measured in specific, mathematical units instead of relative comparisons between objects or arbitrary readings from needles. There was one problem: because no one had measured magnetism in mathematical units before, there were no instruments capable of making the measurements.

To solve this problem, Gauss and Weber invented the gaussmeter (more modernly known as the magnetometer or magnometer) in 1837, an instrument that measured the strength of a magnetic field. With the gaussmeter and gauss unit of measurement, the two could quantify a previously unquantifiable force.

For many decades, the gauss was the standard unit used to measure magnetism, including measurements of earth's magnetic field. Today, it has been replaced by a metric unit called the tesla, named after Nikola Tesla. One tesla is equal to 10,000 gauss. Yet the gauss is still sometimes referred to in work relating to magnets.

Both Gauss and his country recognized that the telegraph could be a powerful communication tool and began discussing its potential in the German states. Gauss and Weber began talking with the national railroad system to construct a telegraph that ran across the country along rail lines. After much discussion, the project was dropped because of the cost. The German states therefore lost the opportunity to be the first to develop a large-scale electrical communication system.

The primitive telegraph at the University of Göttingen worked for twelve years, until it was destroyed by lightening in an 1845 storm, yet few people outside of the region knew of its existence. At the time Göttingen was a relatively small town with fewer than 10,000 people, and Gauss and Weber didn't publish many of the details of its construction. What information was published appeared only in German, so scientists in other countries were slow to learn of its existence.

In 1854, for example, more than twenty years after the telegraph was constructed and only a year before Gauss's death, a foreign scientist wrote to Gauss asking for information on the instrument. The scientist was working to construct a similar device and had just learned that it had already been completed by Gauss and Weber decades earlier. Gauss's response to this letter has never been found.

But in a letter to a friend, Gauss wrote, "important applications of this method could no doubt be made, rebounding to the advantage of society and exciting the wonder of the multitude . . . I believe electromagnetic telegraphy could be brought to a state of perfection and made to assume such proportions as almost to startle the imagination."

Gauss understood the telegraph's importance, but he didn't live long enough to see it put to practical use. By this time Gauss's family life was marked by personality disputes and chronic sickness. Two of his five children had moved to the United States and his wife and mother both suffered from poor health. And a new series of deaths would soon leave Gauss alone with his youngest daughter, Therese, for the rest of his life.

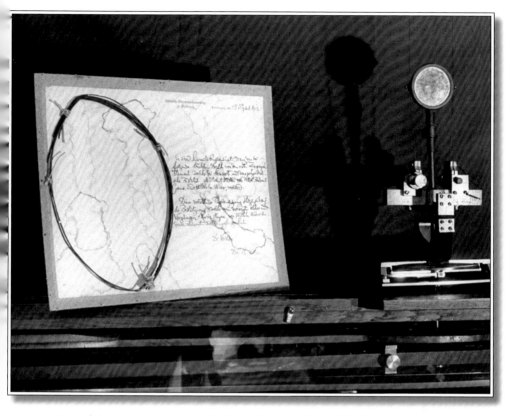

An exhibit at Göttingen's Institute for Geophysics containing the telegraph receiver and a segment of telegraph wire used by Gauss and Weber. *(Courtesy of Walter Sanders/Time Life Pictures/Getty Images)*

In 1831 Gauss's second wife, Minna, died at age forty-three. After this, he fell into a deep depression for a brief time. In a letter to a friend, he wrote, "I have lost all my desire and will to live and do not know whether they will ever return." Minna had been bedridden for many years, most likely with tuberculosis, a common disease of the time. In Minna's last years, Gauss's mother Dorothea was constantly by her side, keeping her company and comfortable.

Young Minna and Therese had helped care for their sick mother for many years. Minna married and moved into her own home in Göttingen in 1830, a year before her stepmother's death. Therese remained in the Gauss home until her mother, father, and grandmother died.

By now Gauss's mother Dorothea had lived in the Gauss home for more than ten years. She maintained her memory and physical strength up until the last months of her life. She died at ninety-seven in 1839.

Dorothea had been Gauss's constant supporter throughout his life, and he knew her life had been less than happy. In letters after Dorothea's death Gauss described her life as "full of thorns," largely because she and Gauss's father were not happily married. Gauss also recognized that his mother was "full of weaknesses."

At about the same time Gauss lost his wife, he lost two close friends and his favorite daughter as well. Gauss's physics colleague Weber and six other professors at the University of Göttingen wrote a petition demanding that the new king of Hanover, Ernst August, reinstate the country's 1833 constitution. The king had replaced the 1833 constitution with the earlier constitution of 1819, so that his son could inherit the throne. (The king's son, it was widely known, was completely blind and therefore could not become king according to the constitution; however, the earlier laws allowed the blind boy to become king.) King Ernst also demanded that all public servants swear a personal oath of allegiance to him.

The "Göttingen Seven" objected to the change in laws. The king was infuriated by the petition and ordered all seven professors immediately fired from the university. Three of the seven were forced to leave the country within three days.

Wilh. Grimm.  Gervinus.  Jac. Grimm.

Weber.  Albrecht.  Ewald.

Dahlmann.

Portraits of the "Göttingen Seven" *(Courtesy of INTERFOTO Pressebildagentur/Alamy)*

Gauss did not add his signature to the petition, as some thought he should, especially given his high profile and considerable influence at the university and in government. But Gauss was not interested in politics. He was sixty years old, and his mother was ninety-five and blind. He did not want to take any actions that might put their lives in jeopardy, or force them to leave Göttingen. And although he considered himself a patriot, Gauss was extremely conservative and disliked what he considered political radicalism. "Political songs are repulsive songs," he once said.

## Gauss and Johann Bolyai

Gauss was greatly admired during his day but even his admirers sometimes complained that he could be cold, insensitive, and aloof. One complaint leveled against him was that he did not reach out to help younger mathematicians, and he did not acknowledge or cite their work. He isolated himself, rather than engaging with his peers. Worse, he was accused of taking credit for other's discoveries. Johann Bolyai, for example, is usually credited as a pioneer of non-Euclidean geometry. Johann was the son of Wolfgang Bolyai, perhaps Gauss's closest friend. In 1831, Johann informed his father that he had constructed a new system which differed from Euclidean geometry. "From nothing I have created a new world." Then in 1832, Gauss wrote a letter to Wolfgang Boylai:

"Now a few words concerning your son's work. If I begin by saying that I cannot judge it, you will be surprised. But I can do nothing else; praise would signify self-praise, since all of the paper's contents, and the way your son has attacked the matter, coincide almost completely with my own reflections which I partly carried out thirty-five years ago. In fact, I am extremely surprised by it. My intention was to leave my own work . . . unpublished during all of my lifetime. . . . I am thus quite surprised that I can spare myself these efforts, and it makes me very happy that it is the son of one of my old friends who has come ahead of me in such a remarkable manner."

Wolfgang Boylai did not take offense at Gauss's letter, but his son was deeply hurt. He waited for Gauss to publicly acknowledge his pioneering breakthrough, but he never did, nor did Gauss ever publish any of his own findings in the same area. Gauss had made an entry in his diary thirty-five years earlier, but he never made a final diary conclusion. As a result it's not entirely clear whether or not Gauss discovered non-Euclidean geometry long before Johann's claim, but it's clear from his diary that Gauss considered the possibility.

Weber returned to Leipzig, in his native Saxony, and found work at another university. This effectively ended Weber and Gauss's collaborative research. Weber eventually returned to Göttingen in 1848, but by this time Gauss was too old to continue scientific work with the same energy.

Another member of the Göttingen Seven was Gauss's son-in-law, who was married to his daughter Minna. He, too, was fired from his job at the university and was forced to move with Minna to another university in Germany. The two left Göttingen in 1837. Three years later young Minna died, causing Gauss much pain. Minna likely died from tuberculosis contracted from her stepmother. Gauss wrote to his son-in-law shortly after Minna's death:

> Even now I cannot realize that my darling angelic child is lost to us on this earth. It was always my dearest, most consoling hope to be reunited with her here, and to see my last years thereby cheered. Now it is gone, this hope! God give us strength to bear the heavy grief. . . . The earth rarely sees such absolutely pure, noble creatures. She was the image of her mother.

That same year, Gauss's lifelong friend and colleague Wilhelm Olbers died as well. Gauss was now an old man with few friends or family. Although Weber had been a regular companion to Gauss, even then Gauss's life had been lonely. A letter from Weber's sister complaining of the long hours spent with Gauss before the move from Göttingen gives some insight into Gauss's approaching loneliness:

> Wilhelm can enjoy Gauss every day as long as he desires. Gauss lives a very lonely life, and Wilhelm is welcome at any hour . . . he has talked with us from 12 to 5 o'clock on all kinds of matters. Recently Wilhelm had Hofrat Gauss for dinner three days in succession.

By this time Gauss was a wealthy and well-known man, yet his two wives, two sons, two friends, and favorite daughter were gone. Only his youngest daughter Therese was left to care for him+. Slowly, Gauss started working less and having more physical problems. The end of life was getting near.

# nine
# Old Passions

**W**ith few remaining family or close work colleagues, Gauss returned to his oldest passions: learning languages, proving pure math, and making astronomical observations.

Gauss decided to teach himself Sanskrit, an old and classical language from India, but became bored and decided to learn Russian instead. Within a year Gauss could read and write Russian fluently, and was the only person in Göttingen that knew the language. His library contained seventy-five Russian volumes, and he liked to read the original works of Russian mathematicians in their native language.

At about the same time, Gauss returned to his purely mathematical roots. His very first professional publication had been a proof of the fundamental theorem of algebra, which he had written to obtain his doctorate degree. The last publication of his lifetime, which he wrote in the last decade of his life, was another proof of the fundamental theorem of algebra, his fourth proof of the theorem.

He began to observe the night sky in his later years as well. The planet Neptune was first discovered in 1846 by one of Gauss's friends; then it disappeared from human view. At the age of sixty-nine, Gauss was one of the first people to rediscover the planet shortly after its initial sighting.

Sometimes it takes many generations to recognize the significance of a scholar's lifetime of work, but Gauss's contributions to math and science were clear many years before his actual death. The list of his memorable discoveries includes: proof of the prime number theorem, creation of number theory, discovery of the Method of Least Squares, drawing of seventeen-sided polygon, calculation of the orbit

Gauss was one of the first people to rediscover Neptune after it was first sighted. *(Courtesy of NASA)*

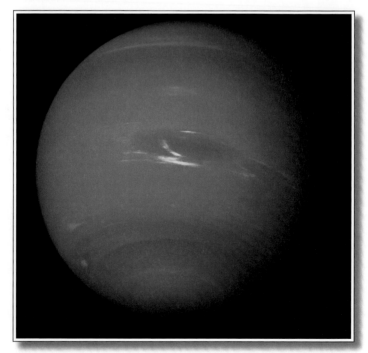

Gauss's image on a 10 Deutsche Mark banknote

of a planet, creation of the Theory of Curved Surfaces, invention of the heliotrope, creation of the new unit of magnetism, invention of the magnometer, and proofs of the Fundamental Theorem of Algebra.

In 1849 Gauss's friends and colleagues at the University of Göttingen held a celebration of the fiftieth anniversary of Gauss's doctorate degree to honor his life's work. Gauss attended and participated in the celebration, though he initially shunned the attention. Gauss also gave a scientific lecture to a standing-room-only crowd, one of many large audiences he addressed during his last years. Even though Gauss described himself as a fairly unimpressive speaker, his appearances drew large, enthusiastic crowds and were always well received.

"I understand that most people do not dream of hearing a lecture on abstract sciences," Gauss explained at one of his final speaking engagements, "In addition to that, I do not pretend to be an impressive speaker. However, I would suggest that even if my topic seems dry to you, you will understand nothing if you do not listen. If, on the other hand, you give me your attention, you might find it interesting." Gauss understood that his work was not necessarily exciting, but he was always confident in its importance. Of Gauss's living children, only Therese attended the anniversary.

Gauss spent most of his final years in his home, reading or writing at his desk. He endured loneliness and pondered life's meaning: "There are questions upon whose answering I should set immeasurably more value than mathematical questions; for example, those concerning ethics, our relation to God, our destiny, and our future; but there solution lies completely beyond our reach and completely outside the area of science."

On February 23, 1855, a little after one o'clock in the morning, a peculiar thing happened: Gauss's pocket watch stopped working. During his lifetime he had carried the watch and wound it religiously. Many good astronomers keep close track of the exact time to make the most precise observations and measurements. Amazingly, the watch had been working well up until this point in Gauss's life. A few minutes after the watch stopped working, Gauss died peacefully in his easy chair, with his hands on his knees and his head to the side. He was seventy-seven years old.

After his death King George V of Hanover honored Gauss with the title of *Princeps mathematicorum*, Prince of Mathematicians.

## Gauss's Journal

More than forty years after Gauss's death, his scientific diary, *Notizenjournal* (Diary of Notes), was discovered. The diary is an important historic document that gives short accounts of many of the brilliant ideas Gauss considered but never published. The notes cover discoveries in geometry, algebra, analysis, and number theory, among others. Written in Latin, the short accounts cover the period from March 30, 1796, to July 9, 1814. One entry appears with an apparently joyous "Eureka!" written in the margin. In this case, Gauss wrote: $\Delta + \Delta + \Delta = N$, where $N$ stands for any whole number and the $\Delta$s stand for triangular numbers.

A triangular number is any number you get by adding up a string of whole numbers in order such as: $1 + 2 + 3 = 6$ or $1 + 2 + 3 + 4 + 5 = 15$. The numbers 6 and 15 are triangular numbers. Gauss realized that every whole number can be written as the sum of no more than three triangular numbers—a discovery worthy of an uncharacteristic "Eureka!"

# timeline

**1777**  Born in Brunswick, duchy of Brunswick (now Germany) on April 30.

**1784**  Enters grade school at St. Katharine's School.

**1788**  Enters high school at the Gymnasium.

**1792**  Enters college at the Brunswick Collegium Carolinum.

**1795**  Enters Göttingen University; writes and uses the Method of Least Squares.

**1796**  Begins diary of math ideas *Notizenjournal;* discovers how to draw a polygon with seventeen sides in a circle using a compass.

**1797**  Discovers the principles on which the proof of the fundamental theorem of algebra is based.

**1799**  Gets PhD degree; dissertation contains his first proof of the fundamental theorem of algebra.

**1801**  Writes a formula for the orbit of a planet; astronomers use it to rediscover the planet Ceres in 1802;  publishes *Disquisitiones Arithmeticae* (the beginning of modern number theory).

**1805**  Marries Johanna Osthoff on October 9.

| 1806 | Son, Joseph, is born on August 21. |
|---|---|
| 1807 | Becomes director of the Göttingen Observatory. |
| 1808 | Daughter, Minna, is born on February 29; father dies on April 14. |
| 1809 | Son, Louis, is born on September 10; wife, Johanna, dies on October 11; publishes *Theoria motus*, major work in astronomy. |
| 1810 | Son, Louis, dies on March 1; marries Minna Waldeck on August 4 (Johanna's best friend). |
| 1811 | Son, Eugene, born on July 29. |
| 1813 | Son, Wilhelm, born on October 23. |
| 1815 | Publishes second proof of the fundamental theorem of algebra. |
| 1816 | Daughter, Therese, born on June 9; publishes third proof of the fundamental theorem of algebra. |
| 1817 | Takes in sick mother. |
| 1819 | Publishes the Method of Least Squares. |
| 1821 | Invents the heliotrope; founding of the magnetic union. |
| 1822 | Wins the Copenhagen University Prize with *Theoria attractionis*. |

| | |
|---|---|
| **1827** | Publishes his memoir on the theory of curved surfaces. |
| **1831** | Wife, Minna, dies on September 12 after long illness. |
| **1833** | Invents the first telegraph with William Weber. |
| **1836** | Invents the bifilar magmetometer. |
| **1838** | Wins the Copley Medal from the Royal Society of London. |
| **1839** | Mother dies; becomes the secretary of the Royal Society of Göttingen. |
| **1840** | Daughter, Minna, dies on August 12. |
| **1848** | Publishes fourth proof of the fundamental theorem of algebra. |
| **1849** | Göttingen friends and colleagues celebrate the fiftieth anniversary of Gauss's doctorate degree. |
| **1855** | Dies on February 23 in Göttingen. |

# Sources

**CHAPTER ONE: Child Genius**

p. 15, "Europe's greatest mathematician," Tord Hall, *Carl Friedrich Gauss,* trans. Albert Froderberg (Cambridge, Mass: MIT Press, 1970), 42.

p. 17, "Father, the reckoning . . ." William L. Schaff, *Carl Friedrich Gauss: Prince of Mathematicians* (New York, NY: Franklin Watts, 1964), 1.

p. 19, *"Liggett se,"* Waldo Dunnington, *Carl Friedrich Gauss: Titan of Science* (New York, NY: The Mathematical Association of America, 2004), 12.

p. 21, "honest . . . coarse," Hall, *Carl Friedrich Gauss,* 2.

p. 22, "find some distinguished . . ." Hall, *Carl Friedrich Gauss,* 6.

**CHAPTER THREE: A Surge of Ideas**

p. 35, "the leading mathematician . . ." Dunnington, *Carl Friedrich Gauss: Titan of Science,* 24.

p. 36, "very modest . . ." W. K. Buhler, *Gauss: A Biographical Study* (New York: Springer-Verlag, 1981), 16.

p. 36, "brotherhood and the banner . . ." "Carl Friedrich Gauss," Academic Kids Online Encyclopedia, http://academickids.com/encyclopedia/index.php/Carl_Friedrich_Gauss.

p. 36, "Through deep reflection . . ." Hall, *Carl Friedrich Gauss,* 23.

p. 36, "It deserves mentioning . . ." Dunnington, *Carl Friedrich Gauss: Titan of Science*, 28.

p. 39, "I shall probably not . . ." Tarrajna Dorsey, "First Thoughts on the Determination on the Orbit of Carl F. Gauss," http://www.wlym.com/~animations/ceres/Interim/interim_tarrajna.html.

p. 39, "future fate," Dunnington, *Carl Friedrich Gauss: Titan of Science*, 32.

**CHAPTER FOUR: Exploring Astronomy**

p. 42, "living for the most part . . ." Dunnington, *Carl Friedrich Gauss: Titan of Science,* 34.

p. 42, "he has explained . . ." Ibid., 35.

p. 42-43, "He desires further . . . usual harlequinery," Ibid.

p. 43, "an excellent geometer . . ." Dunnington, *Carl Friedrich Gauss: Titan of Science,* 36.

p. 45, "I account it the highest . . ." Ibid., 43.

p. 50, "The *Theoria Motus* . . ." Obituary of Charles Frederick Gauss, *Monthly Notices of the Royal Astronomical Society*, 1856, 16:80–83, http://articles.adsabs.harvard.edu//full/seri/MNRAS/0016/0000080.00.html.

**CHAPTER FIVE: Year of Turmoil**

p. 51-52, "Your *Disquisitiones* . . ." Dunnington, *Carl Friedrich Gauss: Titan of Science,* 44.

p. 55-56, "It is the characteristic . . ." Ibid., 413.

p. 57-58, "Since my last letter . . ." Ibid., 62.

**CHAPTER SIX: Changing Direction**

p. 60, "the foremost mathematician . . ." Dunnington, *Carl Friedrich Gauss: Titan of Science,* 251.

p. 63, "Recently I had . . ." Buhler, *Gauss: A Biographical Study,* 53.

p. 65, "How can I describe . . . " Louis L. Bucciarelli and Nancy Dworsky, *Sophie Germain: An Essay in the History of the Theory of Elasticity,* (Dordrecht, Holland: D. Reidel Publishing Company, 1980), 25.

p. 65-66, "This young man . . ." Buhler, *Gauss: A Biographical Study*, 46.

p. 67, "for a professor of mathematics . . ." Hall, *Carl Friedrich Gauss*, 165.

p. 68, "usually he sat . . ." Buhler, *Gauss: A Biographical Study*, 148-149.

p. 69, "The days fly . . ." Ibid, 70.

p. 69, "to gather new strength . . ." Buhler, *Gauss: A Biographical Study*, 66.

p. 70, "throbbing heart . . . and bliss," Ibid., 68.

## CHAPTER SEVEN: Mapping the Earth

p. 80, "all the measurements . . ." Carl Friedrich Gauss, *General Investigations of Curved Surfaces,* trans. Adam Hiltebeitel and James Morehead (Mineola, NY: Dover Publications Inc., 2005), ix.

## CHAPTER EIGHT: Exploring Magnetism

p. 84, "The older she gets . . ." Dunnington, *Carl Friedrich Gauss: Titan of Science*, 363.

p. 88, "important applications of this . . ." Ibid., 149.

p. 89, "I have lost all . . ." Buhler, *Gauss: A Biographical Study*, 119.

p. 92, "political songs . . ." Ibid., 63.

p. 92, "From nothing . . ." Hall, *Carl Friedrich Gauss*, 113.

p. 92-93, "Now a few words . . ." Ibid., 114.

p. 94, "even now I cannot . . ." Ibid., 206.

p. 94, "Wilhelm can enjoy . . ." Ibid, 226.

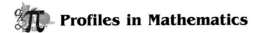 

**CHAPTER NINE: Old Passions**

p. 97-98, "I understand that . . ." M. B. W. Tent, *The Prince of Mathematics: Carl Friedrich Gauss* (Wellesley, MA: A. K. Peters Limited, 2006), 157.

p. 98, "There are questions . . ." Hall, *Carl Friedrich Gauss*, 162.

# Bibliography

Buhler, W. K. *Gauss: A Biographical Study.* Springer-Verlag, New York, NY, 1981.

Dunnington, Waldo. *Carl Friedrich Gauss: Titan of Science.* New York: The Mathematical Association of America, 2004.

Gauss, Carl Friedrich. *General Investigations of Curved Surfaces.* Translated by Adam Hiltebeitel and James Morehead.Mineola, NY: Dover Publications Inc, 2005.

Hall, Tord. *Carl Friedrich Gauss.* Translated by Albert Froderberg. Cambridge, Mass.: MIT Press, 1970.

Schaaf, William L. *Carl Friedrich Gauss: Prince of Mathematicians.* New York: Franklin Watts, 1964.

Tent, M. B. W. *The Prince of Mathematics: Carl Friedrich Gauss.* Wellesley, Mass.: A. K. Peters Limited, 2006.

# Web sites

**http://www.gausschildren.org/cfgauss.htm**
Family Web site maintained by a great-great granddaughter of Carl Gauss.

**http://www.nsula.edu/watson_library/gauss/**
G. Waldo Dunnington's Collection of Gauss Papers. One of the largest collections of personal and scientific papers from Carl Gauss.

**http://www.coloradocollege.edu/Library/SpecialCollections/CenturyChest/ch024aam.htm**
William T. Gauss (an American descendent of Carl Gauss) maintains genealogical documents and newspaper articles about the William T. Gauss family in America on this site.

**http://www.gaussjahr.de/gauss_goe_en.php?navid=2&supnavid=3**
On this Web site you'll find information about Gauss's life and his work at the Göttingen Observatory, as well as information about guided tours of the observatory.

# Glossary

**Corollary**
An idea that follows logically, with little or no proof, from a statement that has been proven.

**Formula**
An advanced mathematical procedure.

**Fundamental theorem of algebra**
Says that for a certain type of equation, the number of solutions is always equal to the highest exponent, or power, of the variable in that equation.

**Heliotrope**
A mapping instrument invented by Gauss that used a small mirror to reflect sunlight over a great distance.

**Method of Least Squares**
A method to take the error out of multiple measurements made by humans.

**Number Theory**
A branch of pure mathematics that concentrates on the properties and patterns of numbers.

**Orbit**
In this case, the elliptical orbit of planets and other objects around the sun.

**Parallel lines**
Lines that point the same direction but never intersect each other.

**Polygon**
A series of line segments connected to form a closed shape.

**Prime number**
A number that can only be evenly divided by 1 and itself.

**Proof**
A demonstration that, given some assumptions, a statement is necessarily true.

**Telegraph**
A device that used magnets and electricity to transmit messages over long distances.

**Thaler**
A silver coin used as currency in Europe for nearly 400 years.

**Theorem**
A mathematical rule that is expressed as a formula.

**Theory of Curved Surfaces**
Says that the curvature of a surface can be determined entirely by measuring angles and lines on that surface.

**Triangular number**
Any number you get by adding up a string of whole numbers in order.

Triangulation
 A method to measure an area of land by laying out an imaginary grid of triangles connected at the sides.

## Mathematical Terms with "Gauss" in their names
Gaussian elimination (linear algebra)
Gaussian primes (number theory)
Gaussian distribution (statistics)
Gauss [unit] (electromagnetism)
Gaussian curvature (differential geometry)
Gaussian quadrature (numerical analysis)
Gauss-Bonnet formula (differential geometry)
Gauss's identity (hypergeometric functions)
Gauss sums (number theory)

# Index